My Brother...
He's an Angel

Written and Illustrated by Savannah L. Leyde

Copyright © 2010 written and illustrated by Savannah Leyde. All rights reserved.
Printed in the United States of America.
No part of this book may be reproduced in any manner
without the written permission of the author except in the case
of brief quotations embodied in critical articles and reviews.

International Standard Book Number: 978-0-9660213-1-8

www.studioZ7.com
Published by Studio Z-7 Publishing
813 Marshall Street NE
Minneapolis, MN 55413-1816

Dedicated to my life's most precious blessings:

Dylan James Douglas
You gave me the strength
I needed to keep moving forward.
Your smile keeps me going.

JennaLee Taylor May
My true Faith and Joy restorer,
Our lives were blessed with you,
when we needed it most.

In Memory of our Angel
Taylor Jeffrey Gerald
You will forever live within our hearts.

To my wonderful husband
Thank you for your continued love and support in all that I do.

Special thanks to everyone in my life who
continously encourages me to reach for the stars.

Far away in Heaven,
way beyond the clouds.
A tiny Angel watches over me,
a tiny Angel smiles down.

There was a time not long ago when Mommy, Daddy and me, awaited his arrival with love, and made plans for our baby.

Together we prepared for him,
created hopes and plans and dreams.
We laughed when we felt him kick,
and thought about the love and joy he'd bring.

Mommy bought me a t-shirt,
I'm the Big Brother, is what it read.
Daddy bought him a matching bib,
I'm the baby brother, is what it said.

Then something unexpected happened, something I did not quite understand. Instead of bringing him home with us, he is now safe in Jesus' hands.

I do not really know what happened,
but it made me sad, I know.
I often think of him,
I would have liked to bring him home.

We do many things together,
to remember him as part of our family.
We made a memorial stepping stone,
and also planted a beautiful tree.

On holidays we hang special ornaments,
sometimes we light his candle bright.
On his birthday we remember him,
and send balloons into the sky.

I like to talk about him,
and often cuddle his teddy bear.
When I draw pictures of my family,
he will always be there.

I send him hugs and kisses,
in my prayers each and every night.
I pray that he is snuggled close,
in Jesus' arms so warm and tight.

Even as our family grows,
he always has a place inside my heart.
Together we will remember him,
we'll never be far apart.

I will remember him always,
and forever wish him well.
I hope he knows he will always be,
my brother, my angel.

Savannah's love and passion for children extends into her career as a Professional Licensed Childcare Provider. Currently holding a Bachelor of Arts Degree in Early Childhood Development, she is the owner and operator of Little People's Daycare and has been providing quality services to local families since October of 2002. Savannah is also a self taught freelance photographer with over five years experience and is the founder of Taylored To You; providing free maternity portrait sessions or birth announcement templates on CD to families who are experiencing a subsequent pregnancy after a loss. Along with her husband, she is hoping to establish this organization in memory of their son who was stillborn in  March of 2007 during the thirty-fifth week of the expectancy. As a freelance artist she also offers custom nursery letters, murals, address rocks and graphic illustrations. Written with personal reflection of her eldest child and how he was able to grieve as a part of their family, and as an individual, Savannah also enjoyed adding a more personal touch, by lovingly illustrating each character to resemble the members of her family. Savannah is a very dedicated wife and mother residing in Minnesota with her husband and their other two children, Dylan 5 and JennaLee 19 months. Written with love for her three beautiful children, and the many infants that pass away each year due to pregnancy complications, health issues, or other adversities. Her hope is that others who have experienced a loss can find this book to be a useful tool in establishing open communication.